Final Exam

FINAL EXAM

Poems by
Andrew Merton

Accents Publishing • Lexington, Kentucky • 2019

Copyright © 2019 by Andrew Merton
All rights reserved

Printed in the United States of America

Accents Publishing
Editor: Katerina Stoykova
Cover Photo: Eliane Meyer (Pixabay License)
Library of Congress Control Number: 2019931062
ISBN: 978-1-936628-48-3
First Edition

accents
publishing

Accents Publishing is an independent press for brilliant voices. For a catalog of current and upcoming titles, please visit us on the Web at

www.accents-publishing.com

CONTENTS

I.

Review of an Unwritten Poem / 3
Windfall / 5
Climate Change / 6
Rabbit Stew / 7
Why Elmer Fudd Does Not Appear in a Poem About Rabbits / 8
What Louie's Been Up To / 9
Cud / 10

II.

A Poet Naps Outdoors / 13
A Warning from the Chipmunk of Doom / 14
B Poem / 15
Cunning Little Fellow / 16
The Elephant / 17
High Dive / 18
Timing / 19
Lost / 20

III.

Yevgeny Yevtushenko Begs to Differ / 23
Quickies / 25
Mistakes / 26
Respect / 27
Why Walruses and Tubas Are Rarely Romantically Linked / 28
Sympathy for the Devil / 29

IV.

Piano Lessons / 33
Feral Pianos / 34
The Anvil and the Steinway Grand / 35
The Lid / 36

V.

This Poem Is Not What You Think / 39
Banana Bread / 40
Terror / 41
Depression / 42
Blind Date / 43
Nothing Is Better than This* / 44
Saved / 45
Percy / 46

VI.

Proposal / 49
The Unreliable Narrator Stacks a Cord of Wood / 50
Advice to Billy Collins from a Concerned Reader / 51
The Full Moon's Consort Regrets an Unintended Consequence / 52
Maritime Trinity / 53
Total Eclipse / 54
Umlaut / 55
Soothsayers, Inc. / 56
The / 57
The End of Civilization as We Know It / 58

VII.

The Chicken Conundrum / 61
Any Poem with Druid Chickens in the Title Is Likely to Succeed, / 63
Never Underestimate the Power of a Chicken / 64
Asterisk* / 65

VIII.

An Interview with the Timekeeper / 69
Vincent, Redux / 70
Three Clergymen of a Certain Age / 71
Satchmo / 72

To Say the Least / 73
Cricket / 74
Final Exam / 75

Acknowledgments / 77

About the Author / 79

For Kirby Andrew Seidel

I.

REVIEW OF AN UNWRITTEN POEM
(after Wislawa Szymborska)

It might have been better
set in Tokyo,
or Johannesburg,
or that small Brooklyn deli
where a bat flew in
during a power outage
in 1946,
causing the first post-war vampire panic.

It might have been better
if the narrator had been younger,
or older,
less omniscient,
more reliable,
Korean,
or not wearing lederhosen.
(What was he thinking?)

It might have been better
as a sestina,
an ode,
a haiku,
a naughty limerick,
or even an epic
in dactylic hexameter
for, as the poet must have known,
there's no such thing as free verse.
Always, in the end, someone must pay.

It might have been better
with crows in a pivotal role,

with an aardvark in the title,
or written by Emily Dickinson.

These caveats notwithstanding,
it must be considered a triumph.

WINDFALL
(Iquitos, Peru, 1961)

A boy sees a truck hit a bump,
jarring loose a sheet of corrugated tin
which severs the neck of a motorcyclist
who, for a time,
continues to guide his bike
with studied expertise.
The truck driver glances in his mirror
and dies of fright.

Though only nine
the boy knows his duty.
Like an ant struggling with a leaf
he drags the metal home.

CLIMATE CHANGE

Black clouds roll in over the old ballfield.
I've come here alone.

I don't like being nine
or being me.

Minutes ago the sky was cartoon blue.
Small birds flocked near second base.

Now they scatter as the wind picks up.
A snake's tongue of lightening flickers,

the thunderhead roaring
like some crazed Norse god.

Rain hammers my face.
Never have I felt such peace.

RABBIT STEW

In my mother's time
the urine of possibly pregnant women
was injected into rabbits.
The rabbit died was code for yes.
I did not learn this from my mother,
whose taste in rabbits ran to Beatrix Potter.
I did learn my first truisms:
rabbits are good
(as in, good versus evil,
not, good,
but even better with Merlot)
and wear waistcoats.
Then came Bugs with his boas and pearls.
So much for truisms.

I shot a rabbit once, when I was a kid in the suburbs.
I fired a .22 from my bedroom window.
As a woman in a New Yorker cartoon,
standing over her husband's body, pistol in hand,
told the police: *I knew it was loaded
but I never dreamed I could hit him.*

At a crossroads in northern New Hampshire there was a sign
that summed up the cony dichotomy nicely:
    Rabbits—Pets or Meat
Those rabbits, at least, had a chance.
Those in service to fertile women did not,
for the code was a lie.
Yes or no,
the rabbit died.

WHY ELMER FUDD DOES NOT APPEAR IN A POEM ABOUT RABBITS

Because Elmer Fudd is not about rabbits, that's why.
Elmer Fudd is about short, bald guys everywhere,
nearsighted guys with speech impediments
just doing what we can to get by,
riding nothing but smiles and shoeshines
and loaded shotguns
while the world slams doors in our faces.
How smart is that?
Attention must be paid!

WHAT LOUIE'S BEEN UP TO

God is not dead. Just ask Louie Bastianelli or any of the guys he plays poker with on Friday nights in the back room of a bar just south of Lodi. The supreme being drops in sometime for a brew and a game of five-card stud. He's a portly gent with a waxed mustache, wearing a three-piece suit. Louie and the guys rib him about that—Whatsamattah, God, white robe at the cleaner's? And God laughs. The stakes are low, dollar ante, and there is an understanding: God checks his omniscience at the door, along with his uppercase pronouns, and in return, the guys don't ask him about his work—about Adam, or the Flood, or God's relationships with his son and the boy's mother, or where God was between 1933 and 1945. Some nights God does all right, but mostly he loses. When it's over, he slips out the back door. Later, when Louie's wife asks him what he's been up to, Louie shrugs, grins: Playin' God.

CUD

An artist draws a cow. Then he draws himself mounted on the cow, and the two of them set off in search of God. The artist looks high and finds nothing. The cow looks low and finds God in a thistle, which she devours, becoming divine in the process. Chagrined, the artist protests that it was he who created the Cow, whereupon She explains to him that he is no longer in the picture.

II.

A POET NAPS OUTDOORS

A poem lurks in the woodpile nearby.
No epic this,
just a modest, striped thing,
lithe, timid,
made to flee.
Now, however,
it glides into the open
and, regarding its creator,
imagines itself a cobra.

A WARNING FROM THE CHIPMUNK OF DOOM

Go ahead and laugh.
But when you have acted badly—
not just badly, unforgivably—

caused your wife, your child,
for God's sake your mother,
pain they will bear always,

like stigmata—
when you have locked yourself away,
a kernel of self-loathing

in a shell hard and small as an acorn—
the last thing you see in this world
will be my shadow.

B POEM

> Poetry is a controlled refinement of sobbing.
> —Paul Chowder, in Nicholson Baker's *The Anthologist*

Not this poem, baby. For starters, check out the cast of characters:
—Bess, a penniless young widow.
—Little Timmy, her brave, blind, nine-year-old son.
—Buster, Little Timmy's faithful guide dog.
—Boris, an oily, mustachioed villain who lusts after Bess and who frames
—Blaine, Bess's true love, now in jail awaiting trial for a murder Boris himself committed.

The poet calls for overacting throughout, and the players oblige. In the climactic scene Boris sneers. Bess gasps. Her bosom heaves. Little Timmy cries out in frustration. Buster bites Boris's ankle. Boris roars in pain, then shakes off Buster and laughs an evil laugh. Just as all seems lost, Blaine, having picked the lock of his jail cell with his toothbrush, a skill he learned while growing up at the Sisters of The Holy Shroud Orphanage near Tombstone, Arizona, storms into the room and, with the strains of Wagner's *Liebestod* swelling in the background, beats Boris to a slimy pulp and forces him to confess his sins. As Bess rushes into Blaine's arms, Little Timmy shouts in amazement, "I can see!" and the credits roll. As you, dear reader, have discovered by now, if it's controlled refinement you're after, you're on the wrong page.

CUNNING LITTLE FELLOW
found poem

> This text was taken, verbatim, from a placard by an antique bird cage on display in the Farnsworth Museum, Rockland, Maine. It was written in 1864 by Fannie Farnsworth, age 11. I have changed only the title (originally "My Canary Bird").

Did you ever see my canary bird?
He's a cunning little fellow.

I think he is a pretty good singer.
He is light yellow.

Sometimes we let him out in the room
and he feels pretty big about it.

I take all the care of him because
he was given to us by a lady.

He has pretty eyes. They are dark brown.
And he is female.

THE ELEPHANT

has left the room,
trunk-in-arm with the 800-pound gorilla.
Still, it would pay to remain vigilant,
given the walrus on the veranda,
the komodo dragon down the hall,
and the imperturbable platypus,
just now laying her eggs
under your bed.

HIGH DIVE

The officials wait at poolside,
along with the real judges:
mother, boyfriend,
sister, cousin.
Each favors a different style,
a different approach.
She takes two steps forward,
leaps,
descends,
a pinwheel,
a swan,
a stiletto
slicing through the surface
to the peaceful depths
where she prefers to stay.

TIMING
(Thursday, May 17, 1962)

My father said goodbye
to my sister and me,
kissed our mother,

and left for work as usual,
wearing a white dress shirt,
a blue and grey striped tie,

a grey herringbone suit,
and black, wing-tipped shoes.
He said he would be home late,

maybe 7:30,
but instead he died at 4:15
according to his brother,

who brought us the news.
While my mother and sister wept
my uncle turned to me:

You're the man of the house now.
The line sounded rehearsed.
Still, in one respect,

the timing was right.
By then I had been eighteen
for almost a week.

LOST

During the winter of 2016,
somewhere in Boston,
a pair of black leather gloves,
a Christmas gift from my mother in 1987,
four months before she died.

III.

YEVGENY YEVTUSHENKO BEGS TO DIFFER

> Without tragedy, you suffer a writer's block.
>
> —Matija Bećković, in the poem "Yevtushenko"

Nonsense. I can do comedy:
Sixteen clowns clamber out
of a broken-down '69 Moskvich 408.
That one, there, with the lavender shoes
and tears painted on his face
climbs the ladder to the tightrope,
pretending to tumble at every step.
Then he executes a hilarious pratfall
face down into the sawdust,
where he remains, dead,
while the crowd roars with laughter.

Or romance:
Before he died the clown was spurned
by the tattooed lady
who cares only for the bearded driver
of the horse-drawn calliope
that amuses the crowd between acts.

Or surrealism:
The dead clown's undoing was a limp clock
with a mustache for hands,
draped over the boa constrictor
of a tightrope.

Or intrigue:
The clown was pushed.

Look, I can even do history:
The dead clown came from a long line

of illustrious dead clowns,
distantly related, it is said,
to the Romanovs.

QUICKIES

In terms of efficiency,
Hemingway's lovemaking

exceeded even his writing.
With him, wrote Martha Gellhorn,

it was *Wham, bam, thank you ma'am,
or maybe just wham bam.*

As an editor, though,
Papa was toughest on himself.

In his quickie with a shotgun,
he deleted even wham.

MISTAKES

> Coming out of the trees was our first mistake.
>
> —Charles Simic

He's wrong about that. Crawling out of the ocean was our initial blunder. Among other horrors, it led to the reptilian brain and the five great extinctions. The tree debacle came later, leading to smog, elevator music, and other forms of pollution. Now that the ocean is rising to reclaim us, it is evident that our biggest evolutionary mistake occurred when we diverged from the branch that blossomed into otters.

RESPECT

Just for a moment let's stop snickering and give them the respect they deserve: walruses.

We've had dogs in space, chimps in space, talking pigs in space, but no walrus. It's time, people.

Here are some signs I have never seen:
BEWARE OF THE WALRUS
I BRAKE FOR WALRUSES
WALRUS CROSSING

On occasion, a certain walrus has been accorded a modicum of respect. I give you Lewis Carrol. I give you John Lennon. Note that each cites not just any walrus, but *The* Walrus. As in *The* Ukraine, or *The* Ohio State University. Perhaps the rest of us should take heed.

WHY WALRUSES AND TUBAS ARE RARELY ROMANTICALLY LINKED

The tuba is the walrus of the orchestra.
The walrus is the tuba of the sea.
The taboo against intrametaphorical marriage is ignored only at great peril.

SYMPATHY FOR THE DEVIL

God has had enough.
At a press conference in Cleveland today,
at the Rock 'n' Roll Hall of Fame,

flanked by Janis Joplin, Jimi Hendrix,
David Bowie, and Thin Elvis,
He said He plans to resign

to pursue other interests:
French cooking, stock car racing, yoga,
and, of course, putting together a band.

He also spoke of writing a memoir
to set the record straight;
several publishers are interested, He said.

Asked about the timing of His announcement,
the soon-to-be former Supreme Being
said that after fourteen billion years

it was time to step aside,
and give the other guy a chance
to run things for a while.

IV.

PIANO LESSONS

There are many things you can teach a piano:
sorrow, grief,
passion, humor, joy,
transcendence, ecstasy, and grace.
But try as you might,
you will never teach a piano
to forgive.

FERAL PIANOS

> Not all Pianos in the Woods
> Had power to mangle me—
>
> —Emily Dickinson*

They come alive at night,
the upright males,
the grand females,

roaming in packs
with their voracious baby grands,
each with powerful legs,

eighty-eight gleaming teeth,
their massive bellies
thundering with hunger.

Beware, brave girl.
If I were you,
I'd take my chances with the bassoons.

---

* From poem #348 in *Complete Poems of Emily Dickinson*

THE ANVIL AND THE STEINWAY GRAND

First cousins, at the very least,
both black,
massive,
resonant,
and liable to fall
from dizzying heights

THE LID

I intend to become
the first garter snake
to master the piano.
It should not be difficult
once I figure out
how to open the lid.

V.

THIS POEM IS NOT WHAT YOU THINK

It is not a blue whale, heavy with calf.

It is neither a virgin nor a Bloody Mary,
nor is it unleavened.

It has little truck with wombats.

When the going gets tough,
the poem starts glowing.

Despite appearances, the poem does not feature
Catherine the Great, El Greco, or Sea Biscuit
in cameo appearances.

It has no interest in tracing its origins back to the Mayflower
or *The Iliad*.

It has never been to Spain,
or slept with the warrior queen Boudicca.

This poem never underestimates the power of a kazoo.

It is no longer contagious.
How could you have thought otherwise?

BANANA BREAD

You wait until midnight. You intend to open the sky's bakery but are drawn instead to the realm of the celestial arachnids. You have always known it was there. Don't worry. Most of the spiders pose no threat, content, as they are, to lay their eggs and suck the juice out of asteroids. The others do not notice you. They have bigger plans, spinning a web from Mars to Venus, the better to catch the Earth next time around. Relax. You still have plenty of time to enjoy a slice of moist and tasty banana bread.

TERROR

Walking fast, a big man turns a corner,
and there she is,
a girl no more than ten,

up ahead,
bent into the wind,
a bulky instrument case

slung over her shoulder.
It's just the two of them
there on the sidewalk,

cold winter sun at their backs.
When his shadow overtakes hers
she turns, eyes wide,

mouth open,
a small gasp.
He flinches.

Then she smiles
and he moves on
as though nothing has happened.

DEPRESSION

You are a cardboard effigy of yourself,
ragged, torn,
left outside a vacant movie house
at midnight in the rain.
You consider it likely
that in the morning some man
will toss you into the back of his truck,
drive you to a field,
prop you up,
and use you for target practice.
You are okay with this.

BLIND DATE

Evie was ash-blonde, pale, a nursing home nurse. She told me about her routine: bathing ruined bodies, emptying bedpans, replacing catheter bags, trying to comfort those beyond comforting. She told me about smells that lingered for days in her lungs, her hair. The night shift was the worst, she said, alone on her floor, praying that no one would die before dawn. I made sympathetic noises. She latched onto these as one might grab at flotsam in a rough sea. A few days later I heard indirectly that Evie would be pleased to see me again, but I did not get around to calling. A week after that, Evie downed a bottle of nursing home Quaaludes and died. A half-century later, I still try to convince myself that there was no way I could have seen it coming.

NOTHING IS BETTER THAN THIS*

* suicide note

SAVED
(Advanced ESL Class, 2016)

for Chun Han Chan

We were talking about logical fallacies.
Here's one, I said:
    —Everything in the Bible is true.
    —The Bible says Noah built an ark.
    —Therefore the story of Noah's ark is true.
Before we continue, I said,
does anyone believe that everything in the Bible is true?
Victoria, the smartest student in the class,
raised her hand like a flag.
I paused, then asked her,
Is your belief based on logic or faith?
Victoria smiled. Faith, she said,
saving me.

PERCY
(Cambridge, England, 2005)

> for Jessica Hendry Nelson

Early morning, a girl
jogging along the riverbank
sees an old man,
standing alone,
staring at nothing,
wearing nothing
but a diaper.
She runs past him,
slows,
stops,
returns,
takes his hand,
says the kindest words
he's heard in years:
Hello luv. What's your name?

VI.

PROPOSAL

In a past life I was a dung beetle
in Macedonia, feasting on the leavings
of the great Bucephalus.
Not a care in the world
until a crow ate me.
Will you marry me?

Two thousand years later
I was a rat feasting on caviar
in the first class galley
of the Titanic.
It was great while it lasted.
Will you marry me?

My most recent reincarnations were cameos:
the bug on the windshield,
the cooked goose,
the toad in the path of the lawnmower.
And now this.
Will you marry me?

You hesitate.
But perhaps I'm getting ahead of myself.
Tell me my darling,
back then,
what in the world were you?

THE UNRELIABLE NARRATOR STACKS A CORD OF WOOD

Your wife said to put down some two-by-fours first because the ground was muddy. Perhaps it was not your wife who said this, but an old man wearing a checkered flannel shirt and a feed cap in a bait shop up in Maine. Perhaps the old man said something different: Ayuh, the bluefish ah runnin' somethin' fee-yus this summah. It is more likely, though, that the remark was made by a cockatoo on a voodoo queen's shoulder, in a café in Havana in the early '50s, and that the fierce runners were rogue toreadors stampeding toward the sea. You remember that you are neither married nor male, and that you would not be able to stack wood without changing out of the little black dress and stilettos you put on for your date tonight in Cairo with the late heavyweight champion John L. Sullivan. Before quitting work you mull over your decision to tell the story in the first person.

ADVICE TO BILLY COLLINS FROM A CONCERNED READER

> For example (and that's the first and last time
> I will ever use those words in a poem) ...
>
> —Billy Collins, in "Good News"

Billy, is it wise to constrain yourself so?
You may regret those words
if, for example,

that man-eating cauliflower
awaiting trial in São Paulo
jumps bail,

or if, for another example,
the stars align themselves in a tableau
of the Virgin Mary nursing twin girls

over Milwaukee,
or if, for a final example,
a unicorn emerges

from that sumptuous beard
you've been growing all these years
in secret.

THE FULL MOON'S CONSORT REGRETS AN UNINTENDED CONSEQUENCE

She looked cold and bare.
I threw my coat over her shoulders.
She shrugged into it gracefully
while down below,
on a park bench in Chicago,
an old man shivered
and, without thinking,
reached for his long-dead wife.

MARITIME TRINITY

We drive east through the night, silent under a cold moon. At the first light of dawn we enter a village on the coast. The place seems deserted. Then an old woman materializes, a grey shawl draped over her shoulders. She is tiny. A black dog twice her size looms beside her. It occurs to me that we must have taken a wrong turn; perhaps we should ask directions? But now, with a crooked finger and a knowing smile, the woman beckons to you. I say we should drive on, she's crazy, but you have already left the car. After a moment you prostrate yourself before her, and kiss her feet. Then, without a backward glance, the three of you turn and walk toward the sea.

TOTAL ECLIPSE

As the disc slides across the sun
its black shadow roars down the hillside

straight at you
at 1,800 miles per hour

and flattens you like a wrecking ball.
You hear a scream,

which, you realize later,
burst from your own throat.

You know only one thing for certain:
It had nothing to do with the moon.

UMLAUT

Ö
A dead colon.
Wide eyes above a gaping mouth,
The Scream writ small.
Rendered aloud, it twists your lips
into the kiss you plant
on the cheek of your least favorite aunt.

SOOTHSAYERS, INC.
Reading entrails since CCLXII

Ninety generations
of fathers, sons,
and holy goats

THE

Genuine article

THE END OF CIVILIZATION AS WE KNOW IT

A plumber's rusted snake in the grass

VII.

THE CHICKEN CONUNDRUM

Why did the chicken cross the road?

That's the wrong question. To determine the right question, we must first identify the chicken.

What chicken?

The chicken, the one that allegedly crossed the road.

All right then: what is known of the chicken?

Until recently, almost nothing. But in October, 2008, archaeologists on a dig near the abbey of Nantes, in France, unearthed a remarkably well-preserved leather satchel that contained a fragmented scroll of parchment upon which was written, in Greek, what appears to be a definitive account of the chicken. According to this document, which has come to be known as the *Kotopoulo* Chronicle,* the chicken lived in the Holy Land at the time of Jesus, and belonged to a family of peasants whose hut and meager barnyard lay in a small valley bisected by the road to Calvary. The document describes the chicken as being unusually large for its time, probably about seven pounds, with black, shiny feathers. On the day of the crucifixion the chicken encountered Jesus amidst the procession of Roman soldiers escorting him to Golgotha. The chicken flapped its wings and flew over the heads of the soldiers, coming to roost on the crossbar of the crucifix. And there the chicken remained throughout the entire ordeal, from the time the cross was anchored in the ground until Jesus drew his last breath.

Why did the soldiers leave the chicken undisturbed?

Perhaps because they saw it as some kind of omen. Or perhaps simply because they planned to eat the bird once their work was done. In the fragmentary remains of the *Chronicle* there is no mention of what became of the chicken following the crucifixion.

* Greek for chicken

Nowhere in the Gospels—or anywhere in the Bible, for that matter—is there any mention of such a chicken.

Not directly. But in Matthew 23:37 Jesus laments, "Oh, Jerusalem, Jerusalem, that killeth the prophets and stoneth them that are sent unto her! How often would I have gathered thy children together, even as a hen gathereth her chickens under her wings, and ye would not!" According to the *Chronicle,* as late as the seventh century, an obscure Irish sect held that this utterance amounted to a prophecy that on the day of the crucifixion, an angel would assume the form of a hen, so that she might watch over both the body and the soul of Jesus.

Then why has there been no acknowledgment of the existence of this holy hen for more than a thousand years?

All seven members of the Irish sect were set upon and slain by militant Druids, to whom their insistence that a divine chicken watched over Jesus amounted to a blasphemous mix of Christianity and pantheism. Thereafter, debate over the significance of the chicken languished as theologians devoted themselves to questions that seemed more pressing at the time, such as the divinity of Mary and the precise natures of Heaven and Hell. Then, at some point in the ninth century, a monk at the abbey of Nantes came across the *Kotopoulo Chronicle.* Unfortunately the monk's Greek was not as strong as his Latin. His attempt to translate the document's seminal inquiry into French resulted in the following sentence: *Pourquoi le poulet al-il traverse la route?*

Which, in turn, was loosely translated into English as, Why did the chicken cross the road?

Precisely. And that is the text that misguided scholars have been pondering for the last millennium, when in fact, had the translation been accurate, or had they had access to the original Greek manuscript, they would have been debating the *real* question raised in the text—the vital yet unexplored matter of why the chicken rode the cross.

ANY POEM WITH DRUID CHICKENS IN THE TITLE IS LIKELY TO SUCCEED,

something that cannot be said for poems
with titles lacking chickens, Druids,
or, worse, both. I mean,
which is going to be more engaging,
a poem titled

What I Did on My Summer Vacation

or a poem titled

What I Did on My Summer Vacation Is as Nothing Compared to What a Few Determined Druid Chickens Pulled off While Scratching Around at Hastings in 1066 or Plymouth Rock in 1620, or Outside the Sun Records Studio in Memphis, Tennessee, in 1956, and Never Mind About the Raven and the Dove, Who Do You Think Laid Those Six Dark Magic Eggs that Kept the Whole Horde on the Ark Fed All Those Weeks in the Rain, Centuries Before Jesus Tried to Pass Off that Loaves and Fishes Trick as His Own, Thus Bringing About the Great Schism that Drove Christians and Druids Apart Forever?

I mean, really.

NEVER UNDERESTIMATE THE POWER OF A CHICKEN

Hard as it is to believe,
there are still people who think the c
in $E = mc^2$
has something to do with light.

ASTERISK*

* the key to everything

VIII.

AN INTERVIEW WITH THE TIMEKEEPER

1. *Who arrives on time?*

   A soldier or a clerk. Beware if either attempts to dismount.

2. *What is the nick of time?*

   A cut too deep to have been made by any scalpel.

3. *How can one make up for lost time?*

   One can't. It is never time that has been lost.

4. *Is it possible to steal a few minutes?*

   The thief is always caught. The penalty is eternal.

5. *What is the best way to kill time?*

   Men use guns. Women prefer poison.

6. *How does now become forever?*

   The time is ripe.
   The time has come.
   Time is the ultimate hermaphrodite.

VINCENT, REDUX

A one-eared sow
toting a silk purse
in which she keeps
a paintbrush.

THREE CLERGYMEN OF A CERTAIN AGE

A rabbi, a priest, and a minister walk into a poem
that, unbeknownst to them, is reserved for women only, among them
Mae West, Ella Fitzgerald, Emily Dickinson, Virginia Woolf,

and Dorothy Parker, who wrote herself into
the second stanza. There is plenty of wine in the poem,
as well as a sufficiency of gin. Several hours pass

as the women talk of theater and art, music and writing,
while the befuddled men look on.
Then the tipsy Parker points and says,

Let's play finish-the-sentence.
When guys like these wander into a poem full of women,
eventually they will:

Come up and see me sometime, says West.
Get a poem of their own, replies Woolf.
Stop for Death, says Dickinson.

But it is Fitzgerald who belts out the last word: Scat.

SATCHMO

On my first night as an angel I joined my new brethren
in their quest for the perfect head of a pin.
In the beginning enthusiasm ran high,
but as we searched in vain
through hundreds of haberdasheries, tailor shops,
and bridal fitting rooms,
the spirits of my colleagues sagged.
We must continue, I said, but they pretended not to hear;
in the end, they settled for the head of a railroad spike,
where they commenced to dance. Between tunes,
Satchmo put an arm around my shoulder.
Happens every night, kid, he said.
Don't let it bother you. Keep in mind,
we may be angels, but we ain't no saints.

TO SAY THE LEAST

CRICKET

Someday someone will write a poem about the time a hedgehog ran out on a cricket pitch in East Anglia during a match, and about the goshawk that swooped down and seized it. Likely it will not be the bowler, whose back was turned; perhaps it will be the wicket-keeper, who saw it all. Or it may be the American university student who was in attendance that day, even though, after all these years, he is still trying to understand the game.

FINAL EXAM

The proctor,
an ancient she-crow,
offers instructions
vague as fog.
You are given to understand
that the allotted time varies,
as does the arc of the grading curve.
There are no right answers
and also, perhaps,
no wrong ones.
In fact, it seems
there are no answers.
All that remain are some fragments
of a single question
scattered on a cave floor
in southwestern France
among the ashes
of a long-dead fire.

ACKNOWLEDGMENTS

My thanks to Kendra Ford, Shelley Girdner, Kimberly Green, Jody Hetherington, and Mekeel McBride, my intrepid writing group, for the tough love they continue to bestow on my work, and to Katerina Stoykova, my editor and publisher for her unwavering encouragement and guidance over the past eight years.

"Cud" appeared in *Closer Readings*, a publication of the Museum of Art at the University of New Hampshire, 2017

"Depression" appeared in the *American Journal of Nursing*, June, 2017

"The Chicken Conundrum" appeared in *The Fiddleback*, 2010

ABOUT THE AUTHOR

Andrew Merton is a journalist, essayist, and poet. Publications in which his nonfiction has appeared include *Esquire, Ms. Magazine, The New York Times Magazine, Boston Magazine,* and *The Boston Globe.* His book *Enemies of Choice: The Right-To-Life Movement and Its Threat to Abortion,* was published by Beacon Press in 1980. His poetry has appeared in *Bellevue Literary Review, Alaska Quarterly Review, The Rialto* (U.K.), *Comstock Review, Louisville Review, Vine Leaves,* the *American Journal of Nursing,* and elsewhere. Merton's book of poetry, *Evidence that We Are Descended from Chairs,* with a foreword by Charles Simic (Accents Publishing, 2012) was named Outstanding Book of Poetry for 2013–2014 by the New Hampshire Writers' Project. His book of poetry *Lost and Found* was also published by Accents Publishing in 2016. He is a professor emeritus of English at the University of New Hampshire.

www.ingramcontent.com/pod-product-compliance
Lightning Source LLC
Chambersburg PA
CBHW020145130526
44591CB00030B/226